Volume 1.

Landlording Made Simple

6 Step Guide to Getting Good Tenants

Dayton Duncan

Copyright © 2019 Dayton Duncan

All rights reserved.

ISBN: 9781079589337

DEDICATION

This book is dedicated to Melanie, Gabby and Dayton (Jr) Duncan. You three give me life and purpose. Every day I strive to do better and to be better for you guys, my family. I loves you.

CONTENTS

I   Introduction   Pg 7

- Landlording
- Highlighted Laws
- Preparation to be a Landlord

1   Step 1: Advertising   Pg 33

- Targeting your Ad: Who is your audience?
- Delivering your Ad: Where to advertise?
- Ad Content: What goes into your Ad?

2   Step 2: Showings   Pg 45

- Property Preparation
- 2 Rules for Showing Properties
- Typical questions that come up during a showing

3   Step 3: Security Deposits & Initial Payments   Pg 55

- The Security Deposit
- Security Deposit Laws
- Security Deposit Refund

- Last Month's Rent

4 Step 4: Screening   Pg 75

- Tenant Indicators
- Tenant Screening Criteria

5 Step 5: Paperwork   Pg 99

- Law to consider when drafting your Paperwork
- The Rental Application
- The Lease Agreement

6 Step 6: The Keys & Final Thoughts   Pg 139

Let's start at the beginning; what is real estate investing and how do you invest in rental properties? Any investment is the fundamental idea of putting your capital towards something with the expectation that it will grow or increase in value. In real estate, the engine that you are investing into is the property. From my investing position, the most common statement I hear non-investors make is, "I want to get started investing in real estate, but I don't know how." There are so many ways to go about investing your money into this space; with 'fix and flips,' rentals, real estate investment trusts (REITs), commercial leasing, wholesaling, probates and more. Before spending a single dollar, I implore you to educate yourself on all of these avenues. If you are completely green and are literally starting from scratch, I recommend that you read my book, "Landlording Made Simple: Buying your 1st Property." (Shameless plug, I know)

My goal with this book is to provide you with some guidance once you have secured your property and are now looking to find reliable tenants. This book will help you navigate the investment landscape and will provide you with actionable steps in securing good tenants in the rental process. Even within the niche of renting there are layers – there are rooming houses, student rentals, family rentals, commercial leasing and seasonal rentals. There are nuances and distinctions to each, but I personally focus on family rentals. I am a guy who has rented and flipped dozens of houses in the Philadelphia area. For over a decade, I have closed deals structured as flips, rentals, refi-cash-outs and wholesales. My preferred avenue of investment is the 'fix and rent' strategy. Oversimplifying it, the goal of a fix and rent is to purchase a property, perform minor renovations, collect rent while it appreciates and then cash out down the road. This strategy fits the mold often referred to as the BRRRR method; buy, repair, rent, refinance and repeat. The intent of a *fix and rent* property is to maximize your potential returns by investing your sweat equity into the property as opposed to buying an already fixed-up place to rent. Hopefully, you can build a portfolio of rental properties that will provide you with long term residual income. The landscape for the rental market is only getting better. The pool of renters is increasing, rental prices are getting better and real estate in general continues to represent a huge portion of the wealth in the country. In fact, rent prices have increased in 91 of the 100 largest cities in the United States over the last year and 37% of households in the US are renting their home. In Pennsylvania, 29% of homes are rented. The number of renters has not been this high since 1965, and according to the US Census Bureau, the recent increase is because more groups are renting that have traditionally not rented, such as adults 45 and older.

Student Rental Property

Success Story Break Down

Purchase Price	$68,400
Down Payment (20%) + Closing Costs	$20,430
Loan Amount	$54,720
Mortgage Payment (includes Taxes & Insurance)	$461
Rehab Costs	$22,500
Total Cash out-of-pocket	$42,930
Monthly Rent	$1,350
Montly Profit	$889

Annual Profit (minus 20% Contingency Loss) = $7,112

*NOTE: This property was a Temple University Student Rental. The leases were 10-month terms (excludes summer months) in an advertisement effort to lock in tenants. The method worked and kept my Temple units fully occupied throughout the 6 years that I owned them.

Student Rental Property

Success Story Break Down

As the student market continued to heat up, I upgraded all of my 3-bedroom houses to 4 bedroom. Adding the extra room allowed me to collect an additional $450 for the house.

Additional Rehab Cost (repairs + add'l bdrm)	$6,500
Total Cash out-of-pocket (updated)	$49,430
Bank Assigned ARV (appraisal value)	$155,000
Refinance Amount (80% ARV)	$124,000
New Mortgage Payment (includes Taxes & Insurance)	$808
Cash Out Amount (Loan - Old Loan - Cash Invested)	$16,350
Monthly Rent	$1,800
Montly Profit	$992

Annual Profit (minus 20% Contingency Loss) = $7,936

- I was able to increase my monthly Cash flow by ~$100
- I got all of my investment money back PLUS an additional $16,350 once I refi'd
- Numbers are a bit higher than your typical rental because this is a student rental

SUCCESS STORY BREAKDOWN

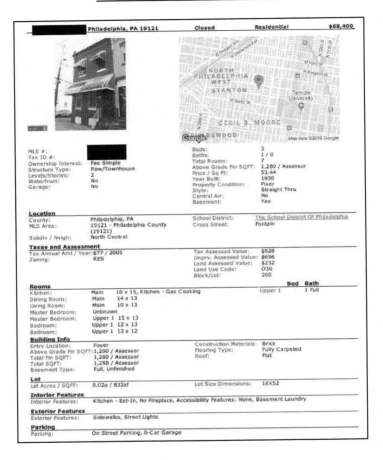

	Philadelphia, PA 19121	Closed	Residential	$68,400

MLS #:		Beds:	3
Tax ID #:		Baths:	1 / 0
Ownership Interest:	Fee Simple	Total Rooms:	7
Structure Type:	Row/Townhouse	Above Grade Fin SQFT:	1,280 / Assessor
Levels/Stories:	2	Price / Sq Ft:	53.44
Waterfront:	No	Year Built:	1930
Garage:	No	Property Condition:	Fixer
		Style:	Straight Thru
		Central Air:	No
		Basement:	Yes

Location
County:	Philadelphia, PA	School District:	The School District Of Philadelphia
MLS Area:	19121 - Philadelphia County (19121)	Cross Street:	Fontain
Subdiv / Neigh:	North Central		

Taxes and Assessment
Tax Annual Amt / Year:	$77 / 2005	Tax Assessed Value:	$928
Zoning:	RES	Imprv. Assessed Value:	$696
		Land Assessed Value:	$232
		Land Use Code:	O30
		Block/Lot:	26D

Rooms
			Bed	Bath
Kitchen:	Main	10 x 15, Kitchen - Gas Cooking	Upper 1	1 Full
Dining Room:	Main	14 x 13		
Living Room:	Main	10 x 13		
Master Bedroom:	Unknown			
Master Bedroom:	Upper 1	15 x 13		
Bedroom:	Upper 1	12 x 13		
Bedroom:	Upper 1	13 x 12		

Building Info
Entry Location:	Foyer	Construction Materials:	Brick
Above Grade Fin SQFT:	1,280 / Assessor	Flooring Type:	Fully Carpeted
Total Fin SQFT:	1,280 / Assessor	Roof:	Flat
Total SQFT:	1,280 / Assessor		
Basement Type:	Full, Unfinished		

Lot
Lot Acres / SQFT:	0.02a / 832sf	Lot Size Dimensions:	16X52

Interior Features
Interior Features: Kitchen - Eat-In, No Fireplace, Accessibility Features: None, Basement Laundry

Exterior Features
Exterior Features: Sidewalks, Street Lights

Parking
Parking: On Street Parking, 0-Car Garage

SUCCESS STORY BREAKDOWN

Utilities
Utilities:	No Cooling, Heating: Forced Air, Heating Fuel: Natural Gas, Hot Water: Natural Gas, Water Source: Public, Sewer: Public Sewer

Remarks
Exclusions:	Tenants Property
Agent:	None
Public:	Large corner property on tree lined street near the University. Currently tenant occupied paying $700 per/month. This property is in need of updating and is being sold in its present AS-IS condition.

Listing Office
Listing Agent:
Listing Agent Email:
Broker of Record:
Listing Office:

Office Phone:
Office Email:

Compensation
Buyer Agency Comp:	3%%	Dual/Var Comm:	No

Listing Details
Original Price:	$74,900	Previous List Price:	$74,900
Vacation Rental:	No	Owner Name:	SEE LISTING AGENT
Listing Agrmnt Type:	Exclusive Right	DOM / CDOM:	100 / 100
Prospects Excluded:	No	Original MLS Name:	TREND
Listing Service Type:	Full Service	Off Market Date:	04/07/06
Dual Agency:	No		
Original MLS Number:			
Listing Term Begins:	11/17/2005		
Listing Entry Date:	11/17/2005		
Possession:	Subject to Existing Lease		

Sale/Lease Contract
Selling Agent:
Selling Agent Email:
Selling Office:

Office Phone:
Concessions:

Concession Remarks:	Seller Assist $3,693.60		
Agreement of Sale Dt:	02/24/06	Close Date:	04/07/06
		Close Price:	$68,400.00
Buyer Financing:	FHA	Last List Price:	$68,400.00

©BRIGHT MLS - All information, regardless of source, should be verified by personal inspection by and/or with the appropriate professional(s). The information is not guaranteed. Measurements are solely for the purpose of marketing, may not be exact, and should not be relied upon for loan, valuation, or other purposes. Copyright 2019. Created 08/17/2021 9:08:51 PM

Landlording.

The two keys to success for your rental property are mastering the job of being a landlord and of course securing quality tenants. It is essential to your time and money that these keys are accomplished. The subsequent chapters are written to provide a framework for landlording with a focus on getting good tenants. "Landlording" is a term that covers quite a bit so it is tough to capture all of the responsibilities. In general, the job of the landlord is to oversee the management and care of the tenants and also the rental property. Interchangeable with the title of "landlord" is the term "property manager." When describing roles and responsibilities, it is common to hear both.

Significant tasks overseen by the landlord include:

- **Getting Tenants into the property**

- Creating & maintaining rental advertisements
- Fielding phone calls
- Preparing the property for showings
- Screening tenants
- Completing initial paperwork
- Creating tenant files & folders
- Collecting Initial deposits

- **Managing Tenants**
  - Handling Security Deposits
  - Handling Rent Payments
  - Ensuring that Tenants are following all property rules
  - Ensuring that tenants are taking care of the property
  - Enforcing any fines, punishments or adverse actions

- Keeping Tenants Happy and comfortable

- **Document Management**
  - Delivering documentation to tenants
  - Processing applications & leases
  - Storing documents securely and archiving documents appropriately
  - Discarding of information appropriately

- **Financial Management & Bookkeeping**
  - Managing business bank accounts
  - Setting rent prices
  - Collecting rent
  - Issuing receipts

- **Handling Property Repairs & Upgrades**
  - Coordinating contractors for repairs (emergent & planned)
  - Fixing minor property repairs (some landlords take on more than others, but a

smaller operation would likely require the landlord to be somewhat handy)
  - Planning and overseeing property upgrades
- **Managing utilities for the property**
- **Staying Legal**
  - Ensure leases, applications and legal documents are up to date
  - Get lawyer's approval for essential documents
  - Ensure all landlord licenses and permits are up to date

Landlording is not necessarily difficult but don't interpret that to mean that it's easy. More accurately phrased is that being a landlord is *straight forward*. The steps are very clear and the implementation of those steps are just as clear. However, successful execution will require preparation, regimented execution, a huge time commitment and constant learning. Your preparation and commitment will set the stage for your success. This preparation includes remaining plugged into the rental trends, national rates, new laws and various financial trends. This can mean the difference between buying an income producing property or buying a money pit. It can mean the difference between buying on the right block versus buying on the wrong block. It can mean the difference between setting rent too high or setting rent appropriately. You must always be plugged into trends, neighborhood changes and property values.

In addition to your preparation efforts to deal with planned problems, you must also be ready to tackle the unexpected problems. You will need to have a solid legal team in place to process your legal documents and/or to assist with the handling of bad tenants. You will need a reliable contractor crew to assist with maintenance issues as well as tenant destroyed properties. You will need to have your policies established in order to address any tenant issues that arise throughout your tenancy. Your preparation efforts will help you to be ready.

SUCCESS STORY BREAKDOWN

Rental Property Rehab

Success Story Break Down

This property was an estate sale that sat vacant for nearly 18months before I bought it. The structure ("the bones") of the house were in good shape, but most of the house required updating. Crunching the numbers, I came up with a budget for each space in the house and began renovations. Once renovated, I expected to generate favorable rents.

The Kitchen

BEFORE **AFTER**

SUCCESS STORY BREAKDOWN

Rental Property Rehab

Item Description	Item Cost	Category Cost
Demo		600
Labor	350	
Dumpster	250	
Framing - Restablize Cabinet Wall	275	275
Electric	560	560
New Outlets - GFCI		
New Outlet - Dedicated Microwave		
New Outlet - Dedicated Dishwasher		
New Outlet - Dedicated Fridge		
Plumbing	750	750
Roughin Sink		
Roughin Fridge Water Line		
Set Sink & Fixtures		
Connect Fridge Line		
Paint	300	300
Sheetrock	250	250
Tile		1,525
Material - accessories	65	
Tile Labor	950	
Floor Tiles	110	
Backsplash	400	
Material		5,455
New Cabinets	1,785	
Countertop - Granite	1,200	
Countertop - Sink & Foucet Addon	350	
Appliances - Stove	525	
Appliances - Fridge	975	
Appliances - Microwave	195	
Appliances - Dish Washer	425	
Door/Window	1,185	1,185
TOTAL COST		**$10,900**

Highlighted Laws.

Two important factors that are heavily tied to the success of a rental are your processes and your documentation. Sticking to your process and thoroughly documenting everything will protect you from many pitfalls. Further, your documentation must be created with the current laws in mind. Therefore, you (or your lawyer) will have to maintain up to date knowledge of landlord-tenant laws. Understanding the applicable laws help me stay legal and avoid unnecessary problems. For example, early on in my investing career I bought a student rental in a neighborhood governed by a city ordinance that prohibited rentals. Not good. Most newer landlords are only concerned with state law, but other laws also come into play. I have since learned to be a lot more thorough in my early vetting and evaluation process. You must be aware of federal, county and local laws as well. Standouts include the handling of security deposits, recourse for nonpayment of rent, fair housing rights and mandates to disclose environmental health hazards, such as lead-based paint. Several federal agencies are tasked with creating and enforcing regulations to continuously improve the rental landscape, such as the U.S. Department of Housing and Urban Development (HUD) and the U.S. Environmental Protection Agency (EPA). At the local level, the city and county often pass ordinances more so geared toward establishing health standards, safety standards, and enforcing antidiscrimination rules.

It is important to highlight the laws surrounding anti-discrimination. At all levels of government, there are laws in place to prohibit you from any form of discrimination when choosing tenants. It is illegal to discriminate in the sale or rental of housing, including against individuals seeking a mortgage or housing assistance, or in other housing-related activities. Mandated by HUD, the Fair Housing Act prohibits discrimination because of race, color, national origin, religion, sex, familial status, or disability. Antidiscrimination does mean that you have to let just anybody rent from you, but it does mean that you must treat everyone fairly (it's kind of a shame that we really need a law to tell us this).

Preparation to be a Landlord

Prior to engaging any prospective tenants, you need to have a few items in place. Successful property management requires all of your systems to be in place as well as the appropriate legal protections. The essential components to establish at the inception of your landlording and property management business are the following:

- **Forms & documents**: Make sure the full complement of documentation you need is drafted, reviewed and readily available. Most crucial documents pertaining to getting tenants into the home are the rental application and the lease agreement. Both are covered in this book.

- **Limited Liability Company (LLC):** Once you begin taking on tenants and establishing your rental efforts as a legitimate business, it's good to formalize it as such. Creating an LLC protects you as the owner and property manger by placing the risk on the business entity. If anything happens, people can drain the business, but they should not be able to target your personal assets.

- **Insurance**: You will need your investment property to be insured. Usually there are packages and deals that you can take advantage of since you are insuring a set of properties (or at least you intend to).

- **Licenses**: Each state has its own licensing requirements for landlords and rental properties; mainly because they want to make money if you are making money. Within Philadelphia, landlords are required to register their rental property; known as the housing rental license. Each property or unit requires a separate license (cost is $50 per property).

- **Maintenance Team**: If you are planning on owning one or more investment property, things will definitely go wrong and break. You should start taking business cards and holding on to reputable references for contractors. The go-to contractors for common issues include plumber, locksmith, handyman and

HVAC guy. These guys can cover the majority of issues that will come up.

- **Business Bank account**: Create a new bank account for your rental business. This is good practice for book keeping as well as tax purposes.

However, all that being said, not everyone is built to manage a property or deal with tenants. And you do not have to. It is important to understand that the management of a rental can be outsourced. There are plenty of management services that you can bring in at a cost of 15% that will deal with all of your tenant and property concerns. The setup and ongoing management of a rental property requires patience and resolve because the journey will inevitably have many ups and downs. It can be extremely stressful and there are certainly risks when dealing with renters. Between continued repairs and the unpredictability of tenants, there are both advantages and disadvantages to rental properties. Disadvantages are rather self-explanatory but some of the advantages include tax breaks, long term equity, and steady monthly income. Regardless, I believe you must enjoy the nuances of being a landlord if you want to take on rentals. For me, property management has been an exciting and enjoyable journey which has brought me much success. I have been refining my landlord machine for over a decade and this book is a record of my tips, tricks and recommended practices for acquiring tenants.

STEP 1: ADVERTISING

The first connection between you and your future tenant is your rental ad. The best way to ensure that you get a good tenant in your property is to meet and evaluate as many applicants as possible. The more applicants that apply, the pickier you can afford to be when choosing who will rent. Your effectiveness in drumming up interest and attracting more applicants is directly based on your advertising campaign. According to data from TransUnion's landlord portal, the average landlord will screen two applicants per rental property. This means that on average, you can expect to take two applicants through your full screening process before you lock in a tenant. Creating a good ad is an important part of the rental process and lucky for you this task can easily be accomplished by shamelessly biting off other successful ads. Simply scroll through other landlord ads and gauge for yourself what you think is effective and what is not. This is your competition after all, so your goal is to put out a better product by learning from them what elements are important. Create your own ad by keeping the good stuff, deleting the crap, and adding anything you think is missing. And voilà, you should end up with a solid rental ad.

Targeting your Ad: Who is your target audience?

Before you begin creating your Ad, take some time to think about who you expect your ideal tenant to be. Who do you think will *want* to rent your property? You will produce a very different ad depending on your tenant market and you must target your ad appropriately based on the specific tenant. The expected tenant will dictate the type of amenities that you choose to highlight and the way you choose to package the material.

Examples of different types of tenants you will find are college students, families, higher priced luxury renters, low income renters (or section 8), singles and young professionals. Consider the prospective tenant, George. George is a 28-year-old finance professional who works in downtown Philadelphia, frequents the Friday happy hour at the *Tavern on Broad*, religiously attends center city sips and never misses Taco Tuesdays at

Drinkers. Then consider Nathan and Kelly Stevenson, who are looking for a home to rent with their 2 young kids. The attractions for single George who is renting by himself are very different from what will be attractive to the Stevenson's and their two young kids. George probably doesn't care about Day Cares or School District whereas that is exactly the kind of thing that the Stevenson's will be looking for. While you want to tailor your ad, it is important to avoid using any discriminating language. For example, do not include wording such as "perfect for families" or "section 8 rental." Instead, you should include amenities and features that support those statements. If it's a family renal, focus on the quiet neighborhood, yard space, room sizes and proximity to childcare. If you are looking for section 8 renters, you can say that "vouchers are accepted."

Delivering your Ad: Where to Advertise?

There are many options of how to deliver your ad, but I almost exclusively go with online ads. There was a time when print ads were the way to go, but nowadays most landlords will tell you that the most effective way to attract potential tenants is through online means. Its quicker and more accessible. There are tons of free (and paid) sites where you can make a post and list your property details. Over the last decade, I have primarily posted my rental ads on Craigslist and I have gotten huge responses. It has been the most effective website and remains to be a free venue. There are other online venues to explore, but some of the other spots require money or warrant a realtor. I see no added value in paying for these services when the free application has proven to be highly effective.

Some of the most common advertisement venues include:

- Flyers & message boards
- Newspapers
- Bandit signs, yard signs & window signs
- Social Media
- Online Websites: Craigslist.com, Apartments.com, Rent.com, Realtor.com, Zillow.com, and the Multiple Listing Service (MLS)

Craigslist is very user friendly for both renters and landlords. As a landlord, all you need to create a craigslist account is an active email address. Once you have an established Craigslist account, an ad can be created and posted on the same day. Your ad can accommodate up to 24 pictures and will remain active for 45 days (or until it is cancelled). Regardless, you should keep your ad live until your property is rented. You should also be refreshing your ad frequently. Older ads get buried below the newer ads so people may not even get to them. If I post something 3 days ago, I might be number 60 or worse on the list. You want to be at the top of the list on the primary days that people are searching. The main traffic days are usually Thursday or Friday, ahead of the weekend. In order to stay relevant, you must refresh your ad weekly or even daily, which essentially means posting a new duplicate ad. This is why you will generally see the same ad posted again and again with the same title and ad description. Unfortunately, this is key in order to keep moving your ad to the top of the heap.

However, if you are adamantly opposed to technology, there are lesser used methods of attracting tenants such as printed ads or bandit signs. Some property owners will still set up signs around the neighborhood or in the window of the property to be rented. This is great way to catch potential tenants as they pass by, and you can assume that they are familiar with the area. However, I would caution that doing this may also bring attention to the fact that the property is vacant. You may attract some unwanted attention, depending on the area you are renting. Early in my landlord career, I posted print ads a lot. When advertising for my student rentals, I would post print ads around campus on message boards and in other high traffic areas. Now that I have transitioned to family rentals, I am exclusively online.

Regardless of how you choose to advertise for your rental property, you will want to monitor the effectiveness of your different ad campaigns. You will likely adopt more than one method so you will want to know what is working. That way you can invest more time and energy into the methods that are most effective in reaching tenants. When people call for showings or to inquire about the property, you should ask them how they heard about the rental. Do more of what works.

Ad Content: What goes into you Ad?

So what goes in to a good rental ad? The ideal post should be short, informative and contain lots of pictures. Most people ignore ads that don't have any pictures. Your pictures should show the space clean, desirably staged and well lit. If you can cost justify it, I'd actually recommend professional pictures for a high quality and professional look. Your ad description should include rent price, security deposit requirements, tenant requirements or restrictions, and availability details. The goal is to be as transparent as possible so that no one will be disappointed or surprised when they go visit your property. Pay attention to key words in your ad title and also your description. This will ensure that you show up on the appropriate searches of the tenants you are looking to attract. It is also a good idea to highlight any bonus amenities such as free internet, free utilities, garage parking, neighborhood (if it's desirable), proximity to public transportation or attractions, and other features of that nature. Whenever I post ads for properties in transitioning neighbors where crime may be a concern, I will highlight the safety features that make my property desirable. For example, my Temple University rental ads would always include the 'close proximity to campus' and the fact that I had security cameras installed. This brought comfort to both students and their parents which ultimately helped me bring in more tenants over my competition. Some people include giveaways in their ads, but I find them to be a bit too gimmicky.

Example Ad:

STEP 2: SHOWINGS

After you get a decent list of interested tenants together, you will need to conduct showings. This is the first impression of you as a potential landlord to prospective tenants. For tenants, the landlord is definitely a factor when they are considering a property to rent. Be pleasant, be confident, and be informed.

Property Preparation.

Prior to walking anyone through, you must make sure all renovations are complete and the house is ready to show. It's also a good idea to have the property professionally cleaned. This is usually a $100- 200 expense, but it is well worth it. If you only have 1 or 2 units and this is not a cost you can afford, then grab your *Fabuloso* and get to cleaning. Either way, make sure the property looks and smells clean. The property should also be well lit and the temperature should be set appropriately so that prospective tenants are comfortable as they walk the property. That means that in the middle of a summer heatwave, you should make sure the AC is on full blast so that everyone's initial reaction is "Ahhh! This feels great." As far as lighting, turn on all lights and/or open all blinds to let in any natural light. The goal is for each space to be inviting.

2 Rules for Showing Properties.

The process of showing the property is fairly straightforward. Your goal is to bring as many people through the property as you can until it is rented. While doing that, you must be a good guide and host to all of the prospective tenants. Like any good salesman, your job is simply to know the product and answer questions. Be available but do not over crowd. If the property is prepared right, it will be received well and should not need your influence to be desirable. I have 2 personal rules that I use when showing properties that make the process seamless:

1. Conduct all showings on a reserved showing day. I actually pick 2 days (a weekend and a weekday). The weekday is my backup day.

2. First come, first serve.

These rules will ensure that you do not run into any headaches when dealing with the plethora of tenant excuses that you will undoubtedly hear. Rule number 1 will absolve you of the scheduling nightmare in trying to accommodate 20-30 different schedules. By holding all showings on 1, at most 2 days, you will force prospective tenants to make the showing appointment important. People who show up are serious and people who don't are not. Being held on a designated day will also scratch the possibility of you being stood up. If you get stood up by 20 people, you are definitely doing something wrong. However, while I hold all my showings on the same day, I still recommend that you reserve time slots for individuals. Stagger the appointments throughout the day because this will put further accountability on the applicant and it allows you time to answer specific questions and provide undivided attention when needed.

Rule number 2 is relatively self-explanatory, but another way that I would phrase it is, "money talks and bullshit walks!" If your property is nice, which it should be, then everyone that walks in will *like* your property. That said, you will again hear a bunch of stories as to how they will get you the deposit money….soon. It is your job to make it very clear to everyone who expresses interest that you will not hold or reserve the property for anyone.

The first person to place their deposit will be first person in line to rent the property. At the time I accept any payment, I issue a receipt (an intent to lease) and I collect an application. If they need time to gather supporting documentation or additional info, I will grant them that time. However, I ALWAYS take an application at the time I accept any money with as much information that they can fill out. This protects both them and me. Also make it clear to the person that the deposit money simply reserves their spot, but it does not guarantee their approval to rent. Let me say that again. COLLECTING MONEY DOES NOT MEAN THE PERSON IS APPROVED! Only the approval process will determine if a person is approved! Please please please do NOT make that mistake. Even as I write that, I cringe a bit because I know someone is not going to listen. I only ask that you read this entire book before you consider NOT listening to me.

On this in particular, I am speaking so emphatically from a place of experience. Every time I have bent the rules or overlooked criteria, it has burned me ten-fold. At a showing for a property years ago, I had a gentleman walk the property and offer to put down the entire year's rent that day, cash. Initially I refused and instead I only took the initial deposit during the walk through to hold his spot. I held the deposit while I conducted a 'fast screen' to get him approved. He failed the financial criteria due to insufficient income, but he continued to claim that his actual income was higher because he ran a cash business. He insisted that some of his income was not documented and he was also able to produce the years rent balance as he originally offered. I foolishly still allowed him to rent and I definitely payed in the end. The story turned into a horror story, as you could image, and I eventually lost money. The story actually ends in a destroyed property, thousands of dollars seized, a double murder and a nation-wide manhunt. Perhaps I'll give the juicy details of this story over a beer (or in the next book).

Typical Questions that come up when showing a property.

As I mentioned, you do not need to oversell your property. Don't be that salesperson. Your job when showing the property is to be knowledgeable and to leave a good impression on all prospective tenants. You should familiarize yourself with all pertinent details of the rental unit so that you are able to quickly and confidentially answer questions. Below are a few typical questions that come up during a walk through:

- How much is it?
- Do you allow pets?
- What utilities do I have to pay?
- How much do I need to put down for security?

- I'll have my security by [*insert later date*]. Can you hold the property for me?

Remember, when answering questions be fair and be consistent. The best way to field questions is to respond with your policy. If asked about pets, respond with your pet policy, "We do not allow pets." When asked about holding a property until they can gather their down payment, respond with my cardinal rule #2, "I'm sorry, but we do not hold properties for anyone. The property is only reserved for the first applicant to pay their deposit." This keeps things simple and very clear. It also helps you to avoid saying anything discriminatory. If you stick to the script, your message will not get misconstrued and you won't get into any awkward conversations.

STEP 3: Security Deposits & Initial Payments

Every landlord will create his/her process for charging and receiving initial deposits. My system requires that tenants pay an initial deposit at the time they wish to reserve their position in line for the property. The property is reserved on a first-come basis, so this is usually paid to me during the showing. I charge a percentage of the full security deposit for this initial payment and then collect the balance of the security deposit once they are screened and approved to rent. This deposit is refundable however, minus the cost of screening, if they fail. As a rule, I will only collect money from one applicant at a time and I always issue a receipt when I do. If an applicant falls through, I go down my list of interested renters and begin the process again with someone new.

The Security Deposit.

Regardless of the amount, every landlord *should* collect a security deposit from their tenants. A security deposit is a sum of money a landlord collects from a tenant to be held as insurance against any unexpected costs incurred by that tenant. Security deposit money protects the landlord against any unexpected damages, cleaning the property, clearing abandoned junk, key replacement or covering back rent. The laws surrounding these deposits vary from state to state but the general premise is the same. You should always collect the entire security deposit before the tenant moves in. If a tenant is not able to provide the full amount up-front, either delay their move-in until the deposit is paid or find another tenant who is able to pay the entire security deposit. Of course, the next prospective tenant needs to be thoroughly screened as well. If you allow a tenant to move-in without paying the security deposit, you are putting yourself at tremendous risk. The most likely scenario is that you will never receive the security deposit, which leaves you financially vulnerable if the tenant causes damage or stops paying their rent. And, it is never a good sign if a tenant is unable to come up with the security deposit when needed. Although you can sue a tenant for any money they owe you, you will rarely collect on that judgement even if it is awarded by the judge. A win is not *really* a win. The security deposit offers you some buffer to soften the blow of the lost money.

Security Deposit Laws.

Landlord-tenant laws in your state provide specific rules for how to handle rent payments, security deposits, and move-in fees. Before engaging in any exchange of money, you need to research your own state laws pertaining to landlords and tenants, so you know how to legally handle and process all payments and deposits. This is important to understand before you set the deposit amount, set the payment structure or determine the holding parameters. Every state within the United States allows a landlord to collect a security deposit from a tenant but most states will dictate the maximum amount you can ask for. Generally, an exact amount is not specified so you are free to set the security deposit as long as it is within the maximum limit. In Pennsylvania, landlords are limited to only charge up to two months' rent for the first year of renting and one month must be returned at the end of the first year. A few states, such as Texas and Illinois, actually have no limit on the amount of security deposit you can collect. That might sound good but remember that you still need to find a tenant to agree to your terms. You don't want to price yourself out of getting any tenants at all. In addition to the statewide rules, you should always check with the city or county where your rental property is located to see if they have conditions on security deposits as well.

Some states require that all references to payments and deposits be captured in your lease. All of these payment amounts should be in writing so regardless of requirement, it is practice including these details in the lease for documentation purposes. This practice should pertain to rent price, details such as where the security deposit is located, and whether you are paying the tenant interest. It is also good to include the banking institution where any deposit money is being held along with any other pertinent details. Of course, all documents should be signed by all parties and dated. Additionally, you should give the tenant a security deposit receipt at the time the payment is made, which should be a separate document from the lease. Certain states will actually require providing separate receipts for payments and sometimes even within a certain time frame of move-in. Some states will go a step further and require you to provide an annual report for the accrued interest on the security deposit to the tenant.

Security Deposit Refund

As a landlord, it is also important to understand tenant rights and responsibilities as they pertain to the deposit money. The tenant must agree with the amount, the general terms and the circumstances of the interest. The tenant should also agree with the landlord on the present condition of the premises. Most landlords will provide a move-in condition report containing a comprehensive list of existing damages. In some states, a condition report must be signed by both parties.

Pennsylvania doesn't require that the landlord provide a move-in condition statement, but it is still a great practice. It is also wise to take detailed notes and pictures of existing damages to capture the general condition. This is especially helpful when it comes to returning deposit funds.

State law also dictates how security refunds are to be handled and the landlord must return the security deposit within a fixed time after the termination of tenancy (30 days in Pennsylvania). At the end of the tenancy, the tenant is expected to provide the landlord a forwarding address to send the deposit and interest, if applicable. The landlord can usually deduct for any unpaid rent or deduct for any reasonable amount necessary to repair damages caused by the tenant. Pet damage can also be deducted. The tenant is responsible for maintaining the apartment in a clean and sanitary condition, free of garbage and bulk trash. However, the tenant does not have to pay for reasonable wear and tear associated with normal use. If the landlord has deducted any money for damages, the landlord is expected to send the tenant a detailed list of the identified damages along with the balance of the security deposit if any exists. The list of damages should include the nature and the extent of the damage, and also the repairs required to remedy them. The landlord should also send any written evidence of the cost incurred such as estimates or invoices. With the photographic support, there is usually little push back from the tenant. Little push back doesn't mean that they like it so you should probably still expect some four-letter words thrown your way. But foul language aside, the documentation usually diffuses any legal action they may want to push. If the landlord fails to return the security deposit, or balance thereof, with accrued interest within the prescribed time after termination of the tenancy then the tenant may sue the landlord.

Example of Security Deposit Refund letter:

Note: *A copy of the move-in/move-out form was attached also when sent to the tenant.*

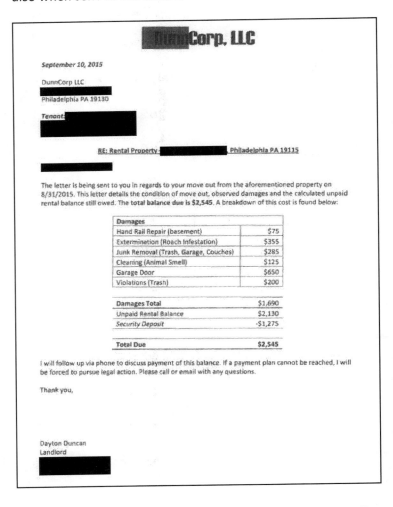

Attachment 1: Photos taken at move-out , 8/31/2015

Roach Infestation:
Roaches have completely infiltrated the entire house. It is apparent that this has been an ongoing issue that was left unchecked. Roaches are in every room and through all of the appliances. Stove, Oven, Washer/Dreyer all had to be replaced. These items were purchased brand new at the beginning of tenancy.

Corp, LLC

Junk Removal:
There was a significant amount of trash and personal property left at the home. It had to be removed and disposed of professionally. These items included dressers, couches, bed frame, furniture, mini-fridge, and bags of trash.

(trash left at Curb)

(trash/junk left in garage)

Corp, LLC

Garage Door:
The garage door was hit my something with force. It is operable but needs to be replaced.

Hand Rail:
The hand rail to basement was broken. It required replacement.

City of Philadelphia
Code Violation Notice

Date: 9/2/13 11:32:59 AM

DURCAN DAYTON

YOU ARE HEREBY NOTIFIED THAT YOU VIOLATED THE FOLLOWING SECTION OF THE PHILADELPHIA CODE.
If payment is not received within 10 calendar days, a $25.00 additional penalty is due.

Violation Code and Description:
10-717(1)(B) - EXCESS WEIGHT OR VOL
Fine Amount: $50.00

You have exceeded the 4 can or 8 bag limit (single unit). No container shall exceed 40lbs.

Officer:

City of Philadelphia
Code Violation Notice

Date: 9/2/13 11:34:38 AM

DURCAN DAYTON

YOU ARE HEREBY NOTIFIED THAT YOU VIOLATED THE FOLLOWING SECTION OF THE PHILADELPHIA CODE.
If payment is not received within 10 calendar days, a $25.00 additional penalty is due.

Violation Code and Description:
10-717(4) - NOT SECURELY BUNDLED
Fine Amount: $50.00

All trash must be tied/bundled or bagged securely.

Officer:

City of Philadelphia
Code Violation Notice

DUNCAN DAYTON

YOU ARE HEREBY NOTIFIED THAT YOU VIOLATED THE FOLLOWING SECTION OF THE PHILADELPHIA CODE
If payment is not received within 30 calendar days, a $25.00 additional penalty is due

Violation Code and Description:
107141 - Premises not litter free
Fine Amount: $50.00

Maintain premises free of litter and debris. In the rear of property.

Officer:

City of Philadelphia
Code Violation Notice

DUNCAN DAYTON

YOU ARE HEREBY NOTIFIED THAT YOU VIOLATED THE FOLLOWING SECTION OF THE PHILADELPHIA CODE
If payment is not received within 30 calendar days, a $25.00 additional penalty is due

Violation Code and Description:
107171C - IMPROPER CONTAINER
Fine Amount: $50.00

Trash must be disposed of in rigid containers or leak-proof bags.

Officer:

Like all document creation in this process, you should recruit an attorney to review and formalize documents related to the security deposit. Especially if funds are being withheld, you should get signoff prior to sending your notification letter. Typically, courts will direct landlord-tenant cases to some sort of lesser arbitration. Having the proper documentation presented the right way will be essential in getting a favorable decision from the courts. If you're involved in a dispute over a security deposit, a real estate lawyer will keep you in the best position to succeed.

Last Month's Rent.

A security deposit and the last month's rent are not the same thing although each is usually equal to one month's rent. In some states, the security deposit actually cannot be greater than one month's rent. *Last month*'s rent is the pre-payment to the landlord for the last month of the tenancy. If the last month's rent is collected, the landlord should also give the tenant a statement indicating whether he or she is entitled to interest. The amount of the last month's rent and of the security deposit is subject to change if the landlord later raises the rent. The landlord reserves the right to increase both the amount of the last month's rent and the amount of the security deposit to equal the new rent. A landlord typically cannot transfer one for the use of the other without the tenant's consent. Likewise, the tenant may not use the security deposit as the last month's rent.

STEP 4: SCREENING

Screening tenants is easy. Following your criteria is the hard part. Most people will meet 75% of your criteria and then they will come up with a story explaining away the questionable 25%. You will develop a set of rules and guidelines that you will use to assess an applicant's worthiness to rent. Put thought into carefully creating your minimum criteria to rent and always be mindful that it is your job to stick to it once that list of requirements is created. Your rental criteria will be personalized to what works for you so landlord rental requirements will vary from landlord to landlord. Ultimately, you are the person that needs to be comfortable with the decisions you make. No pressure but choosing the wrong tenants will make your landlord life HELL.

Although there will, of course, be an official set of rental criteria, but the true process of screening tenants actually begins the moment you make first contact. Prior to your official process, you should be assessing prospective tenants from their phone calls, their interactions during your showing appointment and also during the process of gathering paperwork. You should be making note of the different cues, habits, responsiveness, conversational ability and professionalism. All this will usually expose itself naturally from these initial interactions.

Tenant indicators to pay attention to when assessing tenants:

- Who did they bring with them to the showing appointment?

- Can they hold a proper and professional conversation?
- How do they conduct themselves?
- What is their appearance? Do they look presentable or disheveled?
- Are they clean?
- Do they seem responsible?
- How do they speak? Observe how they talk and what kinds of thing they talk about?
- Are they asking the right questions?
- Do they appear to be drug users? Sight and smells can sometimes give this away.
- Are they or have they been responsive to communications throughout the initial scheduling and screening process?

Although nothing is certain, this impression usually gives you some insight into the kind of person they are and what kind of tenant they will be. I'm not suggesting that you discriminate against anyone or deny anyone the right to see the property (please don't), but you should be taking mental notes of any red flags. For example, they may ask, "Am I allowed to bring my dog?" This is an opportunity to eliminate a tenant that will not pass. If you have a no pet policy, you should reinforce your policy. Hopefully you will deter someone from applying that you would ultimately not rent to. If someone hints that they have poor credit during the walk through, then you should respond with the minimum credit score and credit history requirements. Another example is taking note of the full group accompanying a prospective tenant. If a group of 3 adults walk through your 2 bedroom and you overhear them discussing room assignments that includes their kids then this is a red flag. In a 2 bedroom, your limit may be 3 or 4 people so this would either be an opportunity to reinforce the capacity limits or notate the observation in your files in case they decide to move ahead with the rental process. In this case, you would want to pay extra attention to the formal documentation when they are asked to declare who is living in the house with them.

By the time you get to the official screening process, you should already have a good sense for the person and a gut feeling about their worthiness as a potential tenant. Hopefully, you are able to weed out any poor choices early on and not waste time going through the screening process for someone sure to fail. Again, the process of weeding people out does not mean to deny someone the opportunity to rent because of any prejudice you might have. Specifically, I mean that you can likely deter unqualified applicants from applying by making the minimum criteria abundantly clear. To effectively do this without potentially falling into a discrimination zone, I recommend that you do not offer anything up except your rental criteria. You should not be driving any questioning nor getting into personal details about the tenant. Instead, allow the tenant to speak. Typically, when you allow someone to lead the discussion and you simply listen, they will tell you everything you need to know. Your job isn't to pry and try to extract any "gotcha" information. At the end of the day, any of that information will usually reveal itself throughout the official screening process.

Tenant Screening Criteria

Below I have detailed here the framework around my screening process, but it is by no means gospel. It simply works for me. My screening process is centered around three points which you will find to be common amongst most landlords:

1. Financial standing
2. Criminal Background
3. Tenant History

Ultimately, a tenant's financial standing is an attempt to gauge whether a tenant can afford to live in the property. You are assessing their ability to cover your rent throughout the lease term based on their income and their existing bills. Collect whatever documents and information provides you the comfort that they can do that. Tangible documents that most landlords will ask for to verify income include W2's, tax returns and/or pay stubs. Nationally, rent prices are going up but renter incomes are staying relatively flat, so you need to figure out what income you are comfortable with while also making sure tenants can afford the rent. Although the income requirement amount is completely up to you, the stricter you are with it, the less likely you will be able to find qualified tenants. Typical income requirements are that the monthly household income be greater than or equal to 3 times the rent, although some people allow 2.5 times the rent. This means that if you charge $1,200/month for rent, then the tenant needs to make a minimum of $3,600/month. Also keep in mind that income is verifiable via pay stubs or the W2's so you should never be using stated income. In order to validate expenses, most landlords will pull credit reports. Not only does the credit report validate expenses, it will also show you how the prospective tenant has managed the payment of their bills historically. My process will automatically deny a person if they have any open judgments against them. This is a red flag that speaks to an applicant's disregard for their financial responsibilities. My process does mandate a minimum credit score of 600 but this is something that can be overlooked with a strong explanation by the tenant.

The credit report is such a powerful tool because it provides insight into payment history, expenses, open accounts and delinquent accounts. According to TransUnion's 2017 data, the average renter's 'tenant' score was 650 (equivalent to credit score), which is pretty good by most landlords' standards. Regardless of actual score, it is always a good idea to consider all the information presented in a full credit report and also to review an applicant's eviction history before making the decision. Doing this will hopefully avoid screening out potentially good tenants. Independent landlords have the advantage of adding a more human element to screening which allows more flexibility with the screening process. They can process the additional components of a tenant screen in consideration with the credit score, which can give them the edge over larger property management companies. Remember, the end goal is to predict the outcome of the tenancy, not necessarily to have a certain credit score.

The next point in the screening is the criminal background and watchlist check. There aren't necessarily any financial implications to this screening, but instead it speaks to the comfortability factor. TransUnion data shows that last year, 28% percent of applicants screened had a criminal hit on their record. With 3 out of 10 people likely to have a criminal record, you should anticipate having an applicant with a criminal background and create criteria based on criminal convictions that are of concern to you. Criminal background requirements are very landlord specific because different people will naturally hold different offenses to a higher degree of penalty. This background information is provided to you through a service. The service you select should provide a report to identify the court charge including details, severity and timing of the incident. Your service should also pull from state criminal databases, most wanted databases, and the National Sex Offender Public Registry. As a landlord and property manager, I am registered to a paid online screening service that allows me to package screenings disclosing to me information of convictions, citizenship status, arrests, various government watch lists and much more. In my process, I don't require tenants to be squeaky clean, but I do not bend on sex offenders, child abusers or violent crime offenders. These are immediate fail points for me. As far as I am concerned, these are crimes that speak to the character of the person and I would not be comfortable dealing with a person like that on a regular basis. I'm all about second chances but these particular crimes do not get that benefit, at least not from me.

Tenant history is relatively simple. You will gauge whether that person seems like a good or bad tenant based on their previous rental situations. You will contact previous landlords and ask them a series of questions regarding the applicant's prior tenancy with them. Generally, you will deliver the questions to the previous landlord in a one-page questionnaire but sometimes you will actually go through the questions over the phone with them. In this portion of the screening, you are looking to find out specifics such as payment history, tenant complaints, and general tenant issues. One situation to be mindful of when conducting this screening is the circumstance of the tenant's departure. If a tenant left abruptly due to a previous landlord's neglect or poor property management, the landlord may not provide honest or accurate feedback. Also, if a landlord wasn't prepared for the moveout they may be unhappy about it and could still be harboring those feelings. In these scenarios, the previous landlords may be resentful and disparage the applicant. Try to ask objective questions and sift through any subjectivity or extra hate.

Understanding what information to look for is half of the battle but knowing where to find the data is the other half. There are several services available to landlords to gain access to this information. Most search tools are online and they require a subscription. For landlords who are most comfortable receiving screening data directly from the credit bureaus, TransUnion Smartmove and Experian Connect are two viable options. A few examples of private venues include Lexus Nexus, American Apartment Owners Association (AAOA), TurboTenant and American Tenant Screen (ATS). There are many other versions of these services that you can find with a little research and asking around. All services offer different packages, but I chose an application that is a 'one stop shop.' It allows me to package screenings in an a la carte fashion. Of course, it costs you more money if you want to see more stuff. However, there is no annual fee, but instead charges are billed at the time an application is submitted. This allows me to pass the entire cost onto the tenant at the time of a screening. My service offers detailed credit info, employment verification, watchlists, criminal history along with details of any convictions. It cross-references the applicants name across various national databases and watchlists. This is especially important for me because I auto reject on certain points. As you step through this process a few times, you will develop a strategy that works best for you. Side note, one service that I don't fully trust is employment verification because that is done by basically reaching out to a company direct. If the company is unresponsive, then the findings are reported back to me as inconclusive. I can better find this out through recent pay stubs.

Example Tenant Screening Report:

CONFIDENTIAL

Requested: 02/21/18   Printed: 02/21/18

Background Verification Report   Completed: 02/21/18

Provided To: Dunncorp 1 LLC   Requested By: Dayton Duncan

Subject: **Tony Tenant**   SS #: XXX-XX-XXXX
Address: DOB: 05/21/88
Reference:

CREDIT HISTORY

TRANSUNION CREDIT REPORT

[FOR]   [SUB NAME]   [MKT SUB]   [INFILE]   [DATE]   [TIME]

[SUBJECT]   [SSN]   [BIRTH DATE]
Tenant, Tony B.   165-19-2222   05/88
[CURRENT ADDRESS]   [DATE RPTD]
                                PHILADELPHIA PA. 19120   2/16
[FORMER ADDRESS]
                                  PHILADELPHIA PA. 19141   9/06
                                   PHILADELPHIA PA. 19120
[CURRENT EMPLOYER AND ADDRESS]   [VERF] [RPTD]

                                                                          9/16A   9/16
[FORMER EMPLOYER AND ADDRESS]
Micro-Tech Corp.
                                                                          5/08A   5/08

```
S P E C I A L    M E S S A G E S
***ID MISMATCH ALERT: INPUT SURNAME DOES NOT MATCH FILE SURNAME***
------------------------------------------------------------------
M O D E L    P R O F I L E            * * * A L E R T * * *
***FICO SCORE 4 SCORE +487 : 038, 013, 010, 018*** IN ADDITION TO THE
***FACTORS LISTED ABOVE, THE NUMBER OF INQUIRIES ON THE CONSUMER'S CREDIT
***FILE HAS ADVERSELY AFFECTED THE CREDIT SCORE.
------------------------------------------------------------------
C R E D I T    S U M M A R Y     * * *   T O T A L  F I L E  H I S T O R Y
PR=0 COL=3  NEG=4  HSTNEG=1-1   TRD=6  RVL=4  INST=2  MTG=0  OPN=0  INQ=10
              HIGH CRED   CRED LIM   BALANCE   PAST DUE   MNTHLY PAY   AVAILABLE
REVOLVING:    $1582       $1500      $1486     $0         $30          1%
INSTALLMENT:  $24.1K      $          $10.8K    $0         $397
CLOSED W/BAL:                        $1870     $1870      $
```

Subject: Tenant, Tony B.
Client: Dunncorp 1 LLC

TOTALS:	$25.7K	$1500	$14.2K	$1870	$417	

COLLECTIONS

SUBNAME ACCOUNT#	SUBCODE	ECOA	OPENED VERIFIED	CLOSED	$PLACED BALANCE	CREDITOR REMARKS	MOP
SECURITYCRED	Y 2CLW002	I	6/17 2/18A		$4651 $4651	09 TEMPOE LLC ACCT INFO DSP BY CSM	09B
CREDIT COLL	Y 1GZD005	I	12/16 2/18A		$457 $457	06 PROGRESSIVE PLACED FOR COLLECTIO	09B
LVNV FUNDING	Y 21T9002	I	7/17 1/18A		$164 $164	01 WEBBANK FINGERH PLACED FOR COLLECTIO	09B

TRADES

SUBNAME ACCOUNT# ECOA COLLATRL/LOANTYPE	SUBCODE	OPENED VERFIED CLSD/PD	HIGHCRED CREDLIM BALANCE	TERMS PASTDUE REMARKS	MAXDELQ AMT-MOP	PAYPAT 1-12 PAYPAT 13-24 MO 30/60/90	MOP
CAPITAL ONE I CREDIT CARD	B 1DTV001	3/16 2/18A 7/17F	$486 $300 $486	$486 CLSD BY CRDT GRANTOR	0		R09
WEBBNK/FSTR I INSTAL SALE CONTR	D 2CSN003	12/16 7/17A 7/17F	$175 $0	008M2 $0 PURCH BY OTHER LENDER	0		I09
FST PREMIER I CREDIT CARD	B 41PF045	4/14 3/17A 10/16F	$673 $425 $673	$673 UNPAID BLNC CHRGD OFF	0		R09
FST PREMIER I CREDIT CARD	B 41PF045	6/15 2/17A 10/16F	$711 $400 $711	$711 UNPAID BLNC CHRGD OFF	0		R09
AUTOTRAKK I AUTO LEASE	A 25BF001	2/15 2/18A	$24.1K $10.8K	062M387 $0		111111111111 111111111111 35 0/ 0/ 0	I01
NAVY FCU I CREDIT CARD	Q 692N001	11/15 2/18A	$1582 $1500 $1486	MIN30 $0		211111111111 111111111111 26 1/ 0/ 0	R01

INQUIRIES

DATE	SUBCODE	SUBNAME	TYPE	AMOUNT
1/18/18	BWL3390354(WIL)	BRCLYSBANKDE		
10/30/17	ZNJ0200665(EAS)	VERIZON WIRE		
12/02/16	DMS6367360(WIS)	WEBBNK/FHUT		
9/08/16	FCE3291258(CHI)	DISCOVER FIN		
8/19/16	DMS4941133(WIS)	WEBBNK/FHUT		
6/03/16	FNJ1271865(EAS)	CEL/TIC/CONT		
3/25/16	DMS4941133(WIS)	WEBBNK/FHUT		
3/19/16	BCE2532238(CHI)	CBNA/SEARS		
3/17/16	BNY5894261(EAS)	SYNCB/TOYSDC		

CREDIT REPORT SERVICED BY:
TRANSUNION
2 BALDWIN PLACE, P.O. BOX 1000 CHESTER, PA 19016   800-888-4213
CONSUMER DISCLOSURES CAN BE OBTAINED ONLINE THROUGH TRANSUNION AT:
    HTTP://WWW.TRANSUNION.COM

END OF TRANSUNION REPORT

Subject: Tenant, Tony B.
Client: Dunncorp 1 LLC

Multi-State Criminal

Search on Name Tenant, Tony:

Multistate No Record - No record found: A search was conducted on the multi state criminal database and completed for the above applicant. The database contains millions of records from multiple governmental information sources including court systems, corrections departments, and various other record repositories including national sex offender database. Sex offender searches are limited to what is allowed by each individual state so in many cases only information on high risk offenders is available. This report has its limitations and does not cover all jurisdictions.

Eviction Search

Search on Name Tenant, Tony:

Eviction No Record - A SSN search and an Eviction search were completed nationwide and no records were found. Eviction databases are searched based on the exact name(s) and address(es) you provide to us along with any addresses found on the SSN search. Any variations of names and addresses will effect this search as well as the court access to data that is beyond the control of ATS, Inc.

Additional Addresses Searched:

Address:
  House Number:
  Street Name:
  Street Suffix: RD
  City: PHILADELPHIA
  State: PA
  Zip Code: 19150

Address:
  House Number:
  Street Name:
  Street Suffix: AVE
  City: PHILADELPHIA
  State: PA
  Zip Code: 19141

Address:
  House Number:
  Street Name:
  Street Suffix: BLVD
  City: PHILADELPHIA
  State: PA
  Zip Code: 19120

Address:
  House Number:
  Street Name:
  Street Suffix: ST
  City: PHILADELPHIA

Subject: Tenant, Tony B.
Client: Dunncorp 1 LLC

Page 4

State: PA
Zip Code: 19141

Address:
 House Number:
 Street Name:
 Street Suffix: ST
 City: PHILADELPHIA
 State: PA
 Zip Code: 19140

Message:
 SSN IS VALID. ISSUED IN PA
 IN THE YEAR 1987-1989

DISCLAIMER

Please use the above contact information for any questions regarding this report.

End Of Report

As a veteran landlord, I would encourage you to hold steady to your rules and reject applicants that don't pass your minimum criteria. No exceptions and no budging. Since early on I have maintained my position of failing applicants for certain extreme criminal violations, but unfortunately, I have not always been as strict on income. You will find that every applicant has a story and most applicants will live in the grey area. I come across many applicants that are on the cusp or borderline, whether it's only making 2.8 times the rent or a judgement from 2 years ago that was a "misunderstanding." I once allowed a police officer to rent a property even though his income was just barely below my minimum criteria. I was swayed because he came with good previous rental history and I just assumed he was a decent guy based on his occupation. The situation still made me nervous because my rent was

$1,275 whereas his previous rental, with the glowing recommendations, was only $950. Although the previous landlord reported that he paid his rent consistently and on time, I was still nervous that the few hundred-dollar difference would be too much for him. I was very concerned, but against my better judgement, I allowed him to rent. My concerns were realized, and this tenancy ended in eviction due to nonpayment of rent. My advice to you is to always trust your gut. Ultimately, you need to be the party to make the responsible decision. Not just for your asset but also for the tenant who is becoming increasingly more emotionally attached to the property. You need to make the smart decision so that you don't put the tenant in a compromising position. If they are borderline on the financial criteria then they are a higher risk of having a problem paying rent in the future. Fortunately, it is a landlord's market today. That means there are so many tenants fighting for properties that you can afford to be strict. At my most recent property showing, I hosted 14 people and had 3 people ready to put down a deposit. This is not an outlier, but the norm. I don't need to bend and neither do you. Be choosy and set yourself up for success.

STEP 5: PAPERWORK

Document. Document. Document. Document everything. When it comes to paperwork my advice to you is to stay legal, be extremely thorough and go simple. Renting is not new and there have been thousands of landlords ahead of you renting in your very area. Take their documents and make other people's stuff your own. That does not mean to download someone's lease or application off the internet and to begin using it as your own. What I mean is that you should review templates, wording, syntax, and things of that nature. Get a flavor for inclusions that you like and package something personal based on the examples that are already written. There is absolutely no benefit in reinventing the wheel so you shouldn't be creating anything from scratch. Regardless, once you have pulled everything together that you'd like to include, you should be sending it to your lawyer for review, edits and approval.

To begin my investing and landlord career, I put in many hours educating myself on real estate law and various landlord-tenant rules to follow. Through my research, I was able to take available templates and draft my own rental application and fixed-term lease. I also did significant research online and adopted portions of documents that I found into my own working documents. The benefit of this book and sources like it is that you can digest all of my findings and experiences and skip to what makes sense for you. There are several documents that you will need to be an effective landlord, but this chapter only focuses on the rental application and the lease agreement. These are the two primary documents that will come into play when acquiring new tenants.

Laws to consider when drafting your paperwork.

We briefly discussed the importance of knowing the law earlier, but this is vitally important when drafting your documents and also when requesting information in your rental application. Some federal laws will apply to all, but other mandates and restrictions will be specific to the state (or even the neighborhood). For the purpose of this book, I have provided specific regulations relevant to Pennsylvania laws and PA landlords.

- **<u>Security Deposit Rules:</u>** Recall that you are limited to only charge tenants up to 2x the stated rent. Half of that amount must be returned at the end of the first year of rent. At the end of the tenancy, the security deposit is to be returned within 30 days from the end of the lease or when the tenant officially moves out of the property.

- **Grace Period for Rent Payment:** In PA, there is no regulation around grace period, but it is customary to allow 5 days beyond the due date for tenants.
- **Late fees**: There is no official regulation in PA, but it should be fair. States that enforce regulations on late fees generally cap the amount at 5% of the rent and do not allow it to be charged until at least 5 days has past from the due date.
- **Notice to enter**: You must provide 24-hour notice prior to entering the property. In emergency situations, the landlord may enter immediately.
- **Abandoned Tenant Property:** The landlord is required to hold on to any tenant belongings that were left in the property after the tenant has moved out. The landlord is obligated to notify the tenant, via mail, and allow 10 days for the tenant to claim their items. If the tenant responds, the landlord is obligated to

wait an additional 20 days (total of 30 days) before the items can be discarded.

- **Eviction Process**: In PA, the landlord must start the eviction process by sending the tenant a formal eviction notice (notice to quit). This letter must specify the grounds for the eviction notice, the date that the tenant must vacate the property and any conditions that must be satisfied in order to cancel the notice. Common grounds for eviction, that are legally justified, include nonpayment of rent, violation of terms in the lease or due to damages caused to the property. In Philadelphia, Landlords must allow 10 to 30 days to comply (satisfy violation) or move out from the day the letter is delivered (and received). The time allowed is based on the reason for the eviction action. For example, nonpayment of rent requires a 10-day notice where as significant damage to the property (or similar lease violation) warrants up to 30-days. Once the allotted time has expired, the tenant is formally being told by the landlord to move out. However, that does not give the landlord the right to force them out if they decide not to comply. The landlord will need to begin the legal court process of eviction at this point. As an aside, I'd like to point out that it is illegal to change locks, hire muscle to force tenants out or remove entry doors. The landlord will file a formal eviction lawsuit with the court. It can take up to 6 months to be given a court date, at which time the landlord will present the case to the judge. If the judge rules in favor of the landlord, the landlord must provide the tenant 21 additional days from the court date to vacate the property.

- **Fair Housing**: You cannot discriminate. Period. Therefore, do not use any discriminatory language or ask any discriminatory questions in your paperwork. It is a good idea to include a clause around fair housing in your application and lease.

Based on these laws, and similar, you will want to set your policy to follow all of these tenant mandates. You will also want to add certain inclusions anticipating various outcomes. For example, you may want to include language requiring tenants to be responsible for any legal fees. You may want to include language letting them know what will happen to their stuff it they leave it in the house after move-out. These are just examples of how you should approach the composition of your documents.

The Rental Application.

Often times, the first document that the prospective tenant will fill out is your rental application. The purpose of this document is to capture all personal information, contact details and preliminary screening information from the tenant. Typical inclusions are:

- Name
- Contact Information
- Identifying Information
- Co-Applicant Information (if applicable)
- Previous Address & Reason for Leaving
- Brief Questionnaire
- Job Information
- Income & Savings Detail
- Monthly Expenses
- Non-Discrimination Statement
- Signatures

DunnCorp, LLC

Rental Application

Date of Application: _____

The information collected below will be used to determine whether you qualify as a tenant. All sections must be completed. Applicant hereby authorizes a check of his/her information, references and credit including the use of a credit reporting service. A non-refundable application fee of _____ is to be paid by the applicant(s) at the time the application is completed. A completed and signed application is required for each adult applicant.

1. Applicant's Full Name: _____
    First Name   MI   Last Name

    Previous Name(s) (maiden): _____

    Applicant's Phone #: _____
                        Cell/ Home   Work

    Applicant's Drivers License # / State: _____

    Applicant's Social Security #: _____

2. Co-Applicant's Full Name: _____
    First Name   MI   Last Name

    Co-Applicant's Phone #: _____
                           Cell/ Home   Work

    Co-Applicant's Drivers License # / State: _____

    Co-Applicant's Social Security #: _____

3. Present Address: _____

    Present Landlord: Name: _____

    Address _____

    Period of Residency: From: _____ To: _____ Rent: _____

    Telephone Number: _____

    Reason for Leaving: _____

4. Previous Address: _____

    Previous Landlord: Name: _____

    Address: _____

    Period of Residency: From: _____ To: _____ Rent: _____

    Telephone Number: _____

_____ Initial   Complete Rental Application   1

NOTE: This is NOT a legal document and should not be used as such. The contents of this book are for reference and example purposes only.

DunnCorp, LLC

Reason for Leaving: _____

5. Have eviction proceedings ever been filed against you?   Yes _____   No _____
   If yes, please explain: _____

6. Have ever been sued?   Yes _____   No _____
   If yes, please explain: _____

7. Have ever filed for bankrupcy?   Yes _____   No _____
   If yes, please explain: _____

8. Have ever been convicted of a crime?   Yes _____   No _____
   If yes, please explain: _____

9. Do you Smoke?   Yes _____   No _____

10. Applicant Employment Information:
    Present Employer: _____ Telephone: _____
    Address: _____
    Years at Job: _____ Supervisor: _____
    Job Title: _____ Gross Monthly Income: _____
    Previous Employer: _____ Telephone: _____
    Address: _____
    Years at Job: _____ Supervisor: _____
    Job Title: _____ Gross Monthly Income: _____

11. Co-Applicant Employment Information:
    Present Employer: _____ Telephone: _____
    Address: _____
    Years at Job: _____ Supervisor: _____
    Job Title: _____ Gross Monthly Income: _____

_____ Initial   Complete Rental Application

DunnCorp, LLC

12. Annual Income

Source	Applicant	Co-Applicant	Other Household Members 18 or Older	Total
Salary				
Overtime Pay				
Commissions				
Tips				
Bonuses				
Net Income from Business				
Net Rental Income				
Social Security, SSI, Pensions, Retirement Funds, etc., Received Periodically				
Unemployment Benefits				
Workers Compensation				
Alimony, Child Support				
Welfare Payments				
Other (Specify)				

TOTAL: _____

Assets	Cash Value	Income from Assets	Bank Name	Account Number
Checking Account	$	$		
Checking Account	$	$		
Savings Account	$	$		
Savings Account	$	$		
Stocks / Bonds	$	$		
Other:	$	$		

(The Applicant may provide last three bank statements if Applicant does not wish to disclose Account information)

_____ Initial   Complete Rental Application   3

NOTE: This is NOT a legal document and should not be used as such. The contents of this book are for reference and example purposes only.

DunnCorp, LLC

13. Monthly Expenses:

Obligation	Outstanding Balance	Monthly Payment	Institution Name	Account Number
Car Loan	$	$		
Student Loan	$	$		
Private Loan	$	$		
Major Credit Card	$	$		
Other:	$	$		
Other:	$	$		

14. Household Composition:

List the Head of Household and all members who live in your home. Give the relationship of each family member to the Head of Household.

Member No.	Full Name	Relationship	Age	Social Security Number
Head of HH				
2				
3				
4				
5				
6				
7				

_____ Yes _____ No   Does anyone live with you now who is not listed above?

_____ Yes _____ No   Does anyone plan to live with you in the future who is not listed above?

Please explain if you answer "Yes" to either question above: _____
_____
_____

15. Do you have: Water Bed? Y N

_____ Initial   Complete Rental Application   4

DunnCorp, LLC

Do you have major appliances? Y N   If yes, please describe: _____

Do you own a pet/pets? Y N   If yes, please explain: _____

18. In case of emergency, please notify: _____
Address: _____
Telephone: _____ Relationship: _____

ACKNOWLEDGEMENT OF APPLICANTS:

1. We certify that all information given in this application is true, complete and accurate. We understand that if any of this information is false, misleading or incomplete, the Landlord may decline our application.

2. We authorize the Landlord to make any and all inquiries to verify this information, either directly or through information exchanged now or later with rental and credit screening services, and to contact previous and current landlords or other sources for credit and verification confirmation which may be released to appropriate Federal, State or local agencies.

3. If our application is approved, and move-in occurs, we certify that only those persons listed in this application will occupy the premises, that they will maintain no other place of residence, and that there are no other persons for whom we have, or expect to have, responsibility to provide housing.

4. We agree to notify the Landlord in writing immediately regarding any changes in household address, telephone numbers, income and household composition.

5. We have read and understand the information in this application and agree to comply with such information.

6. We have been notified that the Resident Selection Criteria which summarizes the procedures for processing applications has been explained to us, and we have signed and dated same and received a copy of same.

7. If this application is approved, and move-in occurs, we certify that we will accept and comply with all conditions of occupancy as set forth therein, including specifically all conditions regarding pets, rent, damages and Security Deposits.

8. We authorize management to obtain one or more "consumer reports" as defined in the Fair Credit Reporting Act, 15 U.S.C. Section 1681(d), seeking information on our credit worthiness, credit standing, credit capacity, character, general reputation, personal characteristics, or mode of living.

FAIR CREDIT REPORTING ACT

This is to inform you that as part of our procedure for processing your application, an investigative report may be made whereby information is obtained through personal interviews with third parties -- such as family members, business associates, financial sources, friends, neighbors or other who are acquainted with you. This inquiry includes information as to your character, general reputation, personal characteristics, mode of living, income and credit background. All information you or others give us will be held in strict confidence.

_____ Initial   Complete Rental Application   5

NOTE: *This is NOT a legal document and should not be used as such. The contents of this book are for reference and example purposes only.*

DunnCorp, LLC

We do not discriminate on the basis of race, religion, national origin, color, creed, age, sex, handicap or familial status.

Please be advised that any information given that is falsified in any way will automatically result in the denial of your application.

I/We have read and understand the above.

_____ _____
Applicant Signature   Date

_____ _____
Co-Applicant Signature   Date

_____ _____
Co-Applicant Signature   Date

_____ _____
Co-Applicant Signature   Date

_____ _____
Co-Applicant Signature   Date

DO NOT WRITE BELOW THIS LINE – LANDLORD USE ONLY

Property Address: _____

Monthly Rent: _____ Security Deposit: _____

Application Disposition:

Approved: _____   Approved by: _____
              Date   Landlord Signature

Disapproved: _____ Disapproved by: _____
               Date   Landlord Signature

Reason(s) for Disapproval: _____

_____ Initial   Complete Rental Application

NOTE: *This is NOT a legal document and should not be used as such. The contents of this book are for reference and example purposes only.*

The Lease Agreement.

The lease is perhaps the holy grail of documents that you will need throughout the property management process. The lease should capture every condition and actions associated with the subject rental property. The lease will be kept by the tenant throughout the tenancy for reference of your policies and requirements.

Once I felt educated in the appropriate laws and rule requirements, I packaged my lease agreement. Over the years it has grown and developed. Today it is a thorough and well packaged document that effectively protects me. One early decision I made regarding my lease was to use a 'plain English' format as opposed to legalese. Plain English contracts are written in everyday language (or layman's terms) and should not sound like cryptic lawyer speak. Legalese is a term used to describe contract language that is packed with legal phrases and sounds as if it was written exclusively for lawyers. I saw no benefit in convoluting my messages with confusing lawyer talk. I wanted to use language that was easy to read and easy to understand. I didn't want tenants to be confused about any of my expectations of them.

Example of items to include:

- **Identification of Landlord & Tenant**: In this section, you will formally identify the landlord or property manager as well as the tenant(s).

- **Identification of Premises**: In this section, you will document the property address and any unit specific designation (ex. Appt number).

- **Term of Tenancy**: This section simply states the start and end date of the lease agreement.

- **Payment of Rent**: This section simply documents the rent amount and the day of the month that it is due.

- **Deposits**: This section should describe your security deposit policy as well as document all deposit money that was collected from your tenant.
- **Utilities**: This section should catalog all applicable utilities and clarify who is responsible for paying each. Also describe what documentation you require your tenants to provide in regard to the utilities. For example, I require tenants to provide account numbers and/or a copy of their first bill.
- **Late Charges**: This section describes your policy around late payments. It should describe your penalties, fees and actions that will be taken as a result of late payments.
- **Policy for return Checks & Bank Charges**: This section describes the policy around checks that do not clear and charges that are incurred as a result of the tenant's bank or lack of funds. It should describe your

penalties, fees and actions that will be taken as a result of. As an aside, I recommend that you collect you rent via certified check, money order or direct deposit.

- **Renter's Insurance**: As a property owner or manager, you should consider all of your protections. Renter insurance will protect you from any potential liability issues pertaining to your tenants' personal property within the rental. In this section, you should clearly define your responsibilities and the responsibilities that they are taking on. I also recommend that you require your tenants to carry renter's insurance, but whether you do or don't, it should be clarified in this section.

- **Keys and Locks**: In this section, you should define the parameters and procedures around lost keys, lock outs and the changing of locks.

- **Landlord's Right to Access**: This section details the parameters of the landlords right to access the property. In Pennsylvania, the landlord may enter the property with 24hour notice. In emergency situations, the landlord may enter immediately.

- **Limits on Use and Occupancy**: This clause protects you against unwanted guests. You should include your capacity restrictions in this section and require the tenant to list everyone who is going to be living in the property. Of course, this should fall within your allowable range.

- **Assignment and Subletting**: You will need to include a clause to define your policy on subletting or assigning the property. I do not allow this at all.

- **Existing Property Condition**: I include this clause as additional legal backing that I have provided a property in good shape. This is handy if that ever comes in to question down the road.

- **Tenant Maintenance:** Unfortunately, it is not good enough to just assume that everyone will take care of the property as if it's their own just because they live there. Instead, you will need to define exactly what you expect of them including cleanliness, noise level, and incurred damages. It's also a good idea to call out your expectation for reporting damages, mold, water issues or safety concerns.

- **Repairs and Alterations by Tenant**: You will need to decide what repairs you will allow your tenants to do in the property. Personally, I do not want my tenant making any repairs or major additions to my asset. Unfortunately, when people are forced to pay for something, they sometime are driven by lowest cost rather than quality.

- **Extended Absence by Tenant**: You need to stay plugged in to everything that is happening with your property. As such, you will want to know if it will ever be vacant for an extended period. Vacancies can lead to mechanical issues or break ins.
- **Pets**: You should define you pet policy within this section of your lease.
- **Attachments**: There are several documents that Landlords and property managers will need to deliver to their tenants. These documents can include lead disclosures, additional rules or move-in forms and they should be captured in the lease agreement for record keeping sake. Most property managers have a formal set of rules or guidelines that they require of their tenants. In some cases, the adherence to these rules can impact the tenant's compliance to the lease.

- **Violating Laws and Causing Disturbances**: This is an additional clause that can be added around breaking laws or causing a disturbance. Essentially, a few important rules that are likely already captured in your 'rules and regulations' document are also called out specifically in the lease for the purpose of being documented.

- **Court Costs, Law suites and Attorney Fees**: I hope you never have to go through any of this, but if you ever do, you should assign all financial responsibility of these actions to your tenant. If you don't define this financial responsibility in your lease, you may not be able to charge for it later.

- **Grounds for Termination of Tenancy**: This is a formal statement letting the tenant know that noncompliance to the lease agreement is grounds for termination of the tenancy and they can be removed.

- **Breaking the lease**: Sometimes, tenants need or choose to leave your property and it doesn't coincide with the stated lease end date agreed upon in the lease agreement. You will need to define a policy for tenants who decide to end the lease agreement early. It should describe your penalties, fees and actions that will be taken if this occurs.

- **Validity of Each Part Statement**: This is a formal statement explaining that if any individual part of the contract is found to be or becomes invalid that the rest of the document will remain in effect and will be enforced.

- **Entire Agreement Clause:** This is a typical contract clause validating the entire lease agreement was reviewed and approved by the Landlord and the tenant. This clause also affirms that the agreement is legal and binding.

- **Signatures Page**: the signature page is essentially the page of the document that contains all signatures, identifying information and contact detail. It is a good idea to also include the property address and a notary seal on this page as well.

- **NOTARY Seal:** Leases do not have to be notarized to be considered legal documents but having a notary seal provides an added layer of accountability and legal validity.

Example Lease:

EXAMPLE DOCUMENT

Residential Lease Agreement

THIS IS A LEGAL AGREEMENT BETWEEN THE TENANT AND THE LANDLORD. READ THIS LEASE CAREFULLY BECAUSE TENANT GIVES UP CONSUMER RIGHTS. IF TENANT DOES NOT UNDERSTAND ANY PARTS OF THIS AGREEMENT, SEEK THE HELP OF AN ATTORNEY BEFORE SIGNING.

Clause 1.   Identification of Landlord and Tenant

This Agreement is entered into between _____Dayton's Property Management_____, referred to as the "Landlord," and _____Tony Tenant_____, referred to as the "Tenant(s)."

Clause 2.   Identification of Premises

A) Subject to the terms of this Agreement, Landlord rents to Tenant, and Tenant rents from Landlord, for residential purposes only, the premises located at _____ _____, referred to as "the premises."

B) The following furnishings and appliances are included in this lease agreement: *washing machine, dryer, refrigerator, stove,* _____.

Clause 3.   Term of Tenancy

The initial term of this lease agreement will begin on _____April 1, 2018_____ and ends on _____March 31, 2019_____. After the initial term ends, the Lease Agreement may be renewed if approved by both the Landlord and the Philadelphia Housing Authority (if applicable), unless automatically terminated as permitted by paragraph 23 of this Lease Agreement.

Clause 4.   Payment of Rent

Payment Amount is described below:

Tenant will pay to Landlord a monthly rent of ___$ 1150.00___, which is due by the __1st__ day of each month.

Clause 5.   Late Charges

If the Tenant(s) fails to pay the full amount of his/her rent described in clause 4 by the end of the ___5th___ day of the month, the Landlord will collect a late fee as described below:

EXAMPLE DOCUMENT

A) A fee of __$50.00__ will be charged if rent not paid in full by the __5th__ day of the month.

B) Charges not paid when due become additional rent for the next month's rent.

Clause 6. Return Check and Other Bank Charges

Tenant agrees to pay a fee of __$50.00__ for any check that is not honored by the bank. Landlord reserves the right to require future rent payments in the form of cash, money order, or certified check.

Clause 7. Security Deposit

On signing this Agreement, the Tenant has deposited $ __1150.00__ with the Landlord as a security deposit. When the tenant moves out of the premises, the Landlord, subject to State and local law, may use the Security Deposit, including any interest on the deposit, in accordance with the lease, as reimbursement for any unpaid tenant rent, damages to the property or other amounts that the Tenant owes under this Lease Agreement. If the tenant ends this agreement, the Tenant will be eligible for a refund of the Security Deposit only if the Tenant provides the Landlord with written notification of termination of lease at least 30 days prior of the desired end date.

After the Tenant has moved from the premises completely, the Landlord will inspect the unit and complete another Unit Inspection Report. The Landlord will permit and encourage the Tenant to participate in the inspection.

The Landlord will refund to the Tenant the amount of the Security Deposit less any amount needed to pay the cost of (1) unpaid rent; (2) damages that are not due to normal wear and tear and are not listed on the Unit Inspection Report completed at move-in; (3) charges for late payment of rent, legal fees and returned checks; and (4) charges for unreturned keys. The Landlord will give the Tenant an itemized written statement of the reasons for, and the dollar amount of, any of the security deposit retained by Landlord, along with a check for any deposit balance. The Landlord will refund the amount computed in this paragraph within thirty (30) days after the Tenant permanently moved from the premises, returned possession of the unit to the Landlord and given his/her new address to the Landlord as well as the keys to the unit.

Clause 7a. Deposits PAID

Tenant is required to pay the following prior to move-in:

Security Deposit: Owed $ 1150.00   Paid $ 1150.00

First Month's Rent: Owed $ 1150.00   Paid $ 1150.00

Page 2 of 9   _____ Tenant _____ Tenant

NOTE: This is NOT a legal document and should not be used as such. The contents of this book are for reference and example purposes only.

EXAMPLE DOCUMENT

Total Due: Owed $ 2,300.00   Paid $ 2,300.00

Landlord Signature: _____

Clause 8.   Utilities

A)   Landlord and tenant agree to pay for the utilities and services listed below:

	LANDLORD PAYS	TENANT PAYS
Cable TV		X
Condominium Fee	N/A	N/A
Cold Water	X	
Electricity		X
Gas		X
Oil Heat	X	
Heater Maintenance Contract	X	
Hot Water	X	
Lawn and Shrubbery Care		X
Oil	X	
Parking Fee	N/A	N/A
Sewer	X	
Snow Removal		X
Normal Trash Collection	X	
Other		

B)   Tenant must provide *account numbers* and written proof of all accounts listed above that are paid by the Tenant.

C)   Nonpayment of any bill is a violation of this agreement and reserves landlord the right to force tenant out of the premises.

Clause 9.   Limits on Use and Occupancy

The premises are to be used only as a private residence for Tenant(s) listed in Clause 1 of this Agreement, and their minor children. **No more than 5 individuals are allowed to reside in this residence.** The composition of the family residing in the premises must and has been approved by Philadelphia Housing Authority (if applicable) is as follows:

_____   _____
_____   _____
_____   _____
_____   _____

EXAMPLE DOCUMENT

Anyone not listed above is not permitted to reside in the premises. Occupancy by guests for more than ___5___ consecutive days ___ is prohibited without Landlord's written consent and will be considered a breach of this Agreement.

Clause 10. Assignment and Subletting

Tenant will not sublet any part of the premises or assign this Agreement without the prior written consent of Landlord.

Clause 11. Condition of the Premises

By signing this Lease Agreement, the Tenant acknowledges that the premises are safe, clean and in good condition. The Tenant agrees that all appliances and equipment in the unit are in good working order, except as described on the <u>Unit Inspection Report</u>. The Tenant also agrees that the Landlord has made no promises to decorate, alter, repair or improve the unit, except as listed on the <u>Unit Inspection Form</u>.

Clause 12. Tenant's Maintenance Responsibilities

Tenant will:

A) Keep the premises clean, sanitary and in good condition and, upon termination of the tenancy, return the premises to the Landlord in a condition identical to that which existed when Tenant took occupancy, except for *ordinary* wear and tear.

B) Immediately notify Landlord of any defects or dangerous conditions in and about the premises of which the tenant becomes aware.

C) Reimburse Landlord, on demand by Landlord, for the cost of any repairs to the premises damaged by Tenant or Tenant's guests or business invitees.

D) Be responsible for all minor maintenance and upkeep of the premises. Landlord is ONLY responsible for repairing and servicing major appliance, plumbing, electrical and/or structural issues. Landlord responsibilities are outlined in the <u>Landlord Repair and Maintenance Responsibilities addendum</u>.

Immediate damage caused to the property by the Tenant will be fixed and if necessary items will be replaced. This is done at the expense of the Tenant.

_____ Tenant _____ Tenant

NOTE: *This is NOT a legal document and should not be used as such. The contents of this book are for reference and example purposes only.*

EXAMPLE DOCUMENT

Clause 13. Repairs and Alterations by Tenant

A) Except as provided by law, or as authorized by prior written consent of Landlord, Tenant will not make any repairs or alterations to the premises, including nailing holes in walls or painting the rental unit.

B) Tenant will not, without Landlord's written consent, alter, re-key or install any locks to the premises or install or alter any burglar alarm system. Tenant will provide Landlord with a key or keys capable of unlocking all such re-keyed or new locks as well as instructions on how to disarm any altered or new burglar alarm system.

Clause 14. Keys and Locks

The Tenant agrees not to install any additional or different locks or gates on any doors or windows without the written permission of the Landlord. If the Landlord approves the Tenant's request to install such locks, the Tenant agrees to provide the Landlord with a key for each lock. When this Lease Agreement ends, the Tenant agrees to return all keys to the dwelling unit to the Landlord. The Landlord may charge the Tenant ___$15.00___ for each key not returned.

  a) If Tenant contacts Landlord to unlock a door between 9 AM and 7 PM Monday through Friday, the cost is $ _25.00_. If Tenant contacts Landlord during any other hours, the cost is $ _50.00_.
  b) If Tenant decides to use a locksmith, Tenant must pay locksmith and provide Landlord with a new key immediately.
  c) If Tenant contacts Landlord to replace a lost key, the cost is $ _25.00_ per key.

Clause 15. Violating Laws and Causing Disturbances

Tenant is entitled to quiet enjoyment of the premises. Tenant and guests or invitees will not use the premises or adjacent areas in such a way as to:

A) Violate any law or ordinance, including laws prohibiting the use, possession or sale of illegal drugs.

B) Commit waste (severe property damage)

C) Create a nuisance by annoying, disturbing, inconveniencing or interfering with the quiet enjoyment and peace and quiet of any other tenant or nearby resident.

Clause 16. Pets

No animal, bird or other pet will be kept without written consent from the Landlord.

EXAMPLE DOCUMENT

Clause 17. **Landlord's Right to Access**

Landlord or Landlord's agents may enter the premises immediately in the event of an emergency, to make repairs or improvements or to show the premises to prospective buyers or tenants. Landlord may also enter the premises to conduct scheduled inspections to check for safety or maintenance problems. Site inspections will be conducted every __30 days__. Except in the case of emergency, Tenant's abandonment of the premises, court order, or where it is impartial to do so, Landlord shall give Tenant __24hours__ notice before entering.

Clause 18. **Extended Absence by Tenant**

Tenant will notify Landlord in advance if Tenant will be away from the premises for 14 or more consecutive days. During such absence, Landlord may enter the premises at times reasonably necessary to maintain the property and inspect for repairs.

Clause 19. **Possession of the Premises**

A) *Tenants failure to take possession.*
   If, after signing this Agreement, Tenant fails to take possession of the premises, Tenant will still be responsible for paying rent and complying with all other terms of this Agreement.

B) *Landlord's failure to deliver possession*
   If Landlord is unable to deliver possession of the premises to Tenant for any reason not within Landlord's control, including, but not limited to, partial or complete destruction of the premises, Tenant will have the right to terminate this Agreement upon proper notice as required by law. In such event, Landlord's liability to Tenant will be limited to the return of all sums previously paid by Tenant to Landlord.

Clause 20. **Payment of Court Costs and Attorney Fees in a Lawsuit**

In any action or legal proceeding to enforce any part of this Agreement, Tenant shall pay all attorney fees and court costs.

Clause 21. **Insurance**

A) Landlord agrees to carry fire and liability insurance on the building. Landlord does not insure Tenant's personal property under his insurance policy. Landlord is not responsible for loss, theft, or damage to property of Tenant or Tenant's guests. Landlord is not responsible for any liability or injury to any person while on the leased property. All belongings left by Tenant become Landlord's property to remove or keep as abandoned property. The cost of disposal is charged to Tenant.

_____ Tenant _____ Tenant

NOTE: This is NOT a legal document and should not be used as such. The contents of this book are for reference and example purposes only.

EXAMPLE DOCUMENT

B) Landlord requires Tenant to carry fire and liability insurance to protect Tenant, Tenant's personal property, and his guests. <u>Tenant agrees to list Landlord as additional insured on any policy Tenant purchases.</u>

C) If there is any loss of property by fire, theft, burglary, or any other means, Tenant agrees to relieve Landlord from all responsibility. Tenant agrees to pay for any loss or claims filed.

Clause 22.   Grounds for Termination of Tenancy

The failure of Tenant or Tenant's guests or invitees to comply with any term of this Agreement is grounds for termination of the tenancy, with appropriate notice to Tenant Procedures as required by law.

Clause 23.   Tenant Termination of Lease Agreement

If Tenant chooses to end this lease agreement before the lease end date declared in *Clause 3*, Tenant must comply with the following:

A) Give Landlord thirty (30) days written notice to cancel lease. This notice begins on the first day of the month following the date the landlord receives the notice.

B) Pay termination fee equal to __$500.00__ .

C) Tenant will receive security deposit back, minus damages, if any remains. This payment will be returned within thirty (30) days of move-out or lease end; whichever date is later.

Clause 24.   Attachments to this Agreement

The Tenant certifies that he/she has received a copy of this Agreement and the following Attachments to this Agreement and understands that these Attachments are part of this Agreement.

YES   NO

_____ _____ a.   Attachment No. 1: Property Rules and Regulations
_____ _____ b.   Attachment No. 2: Unit Inspection Report.
_____ _____ c.   Attachment No. 3: Lead-Base Paint Notification.
_____ _____ d.   Attachment No. 4: Landlord Repair and Maintenance
                                    Responsibilities addendum

Please initial as acknowledgment of receipt of the above docs: _____

EXAMPLE DOCUMENT

Clause 25.   Authority to Receive Legal Papers

The Landlord, any person managing the premises, and anyone designated by the Landlord are authorized to accept service of process and receive other notices and demands, which may be delivered to the **Landlord** at the following address:

    1234 Main Street
    Philadelphia, PA 19100

Clause 26.   Validity of Each Part

If any portion of this Agreement is held to be invalid, its invalidity will not affect the validity or enforceability of any other provision of this Agreement.

Clause 27.   Entire Agreement

This document constitutes the entire Agreement between the parties, and no promises or representations, other than those contained here and those implied by law, have been made by the Landlord or Tenant. Any modifications to this Agreement must be in writing signed by Landlord and Tenant. If any Court declares a particular provision of this Agreement to be invalid or illegal, all other terms of the Agreement will remain in effect and both the Landlord and the Tenant will continue to be bound by them.

Page 8 of 9 _____ Tenant _____ Tenant

NOTE: *This is NOT a legal document and should not be used as such. The contents of this book are for reference and example purposes only.*

EXAMPLE DOCUMENT

Lease Signatures Page: RE 1234 Main Street Philadelphia PA 19100

_____ _____ _____
Date   Dayton Duncan, Representative of DunnCorp1   Title

_____
Street Address (of Landlord)

_____   555-555-5555
City, State & Zip   Phone

_____ _____ _____
Date   Tenant 1 Print Name   Phone

                     _____ _____
                     Tenant 1 Signature   Tenant 1 SSN

_____ _____ _____
Date   Tenant 2 Print Name   Phone

                     _____ _____
                     Tenant 2 Signature   Tenant 2 SSN

NOTARY:

COMMONWEALTH OF _____
COUNTY OF _____   SS.

On the _____ day of _____ 2015, before me, the undersigned officer, personally appeared Dayton Duncan (Landlord) and Tony Tenant (Tenant) known to me (or satisfactorily proven) to be the person whose names are subscribed to the within instrument, and have acknowledged that they executed the same for the purposes herein contained, and desired the same might be recorded as such.

IN WITNESS WHEREOF, I have hereunto set my hand and official seal.

MY COMMISSION EXPIRES:

                                              _____
                                              NOTARY PUBLIC

Page 9 of 9   _____ Tenant _____ Tenant

NOTE: *This is NOT a legal document and should not be used as such. The contents of this book are for reference and example purposes only.*

As you create your lease and rental application, I encourage you to gather as much information as you can from other sources and then take the parts you like. You are your own entity and will need to craft your own documentation. Do it the best way you see fit. You must decide between plain English or legalese. You must also decide what clauses you'd like to include. When packaging your lease material, you must also decide on the term durations and the format. Typical term leases are 1 year or 2 years, but some may be as short as 6 months. Others can even be drafted indefinitely, but there are specific rules to each that you should discuss with a real estate lawyer. You also have the option of how you format the lease as it pertains to the clauses and inclusions. You can create a shorter, more abbreviated style of lease or you can create a longer version. Of course, there are some points that are required to be captured in your lease, but others are completely discretionary and up to the individual landlord or property manager. The longer version leases will have every scenario and situation listed as a separate clause. All of this would be within one document as opposed to the shorter version that includes only the essential information such as parties involved, rent price and lease term. All other details would be attached as addendums that would be called out within the lease. Regardless of your choice, the common theme is to have the final document reviewed by a lawyer. It is critical to have a real estate lawyer as a part of your team and he/she should be reviewing all your legal documents. The final component that I urge to include (but is not required) is having a notary seal. I have everything notarized simply because it formalizes things and it makes the document hold more weight.

Remember that there are many other important documents also, but the lease and the application are usually the most critical. Some of the other documents that you will need to manage tenants are payment receipts, security deposit receipt, tenant rules, repair cost guide, maintenance forms, condition reports, monthly statements and an emergency contact hot list. Some states mandate that landlords provide various disclosures as well – lead disclosure, list of landlord's nonrefundable fees, flood zone disclosure, smoking policy, and others. Another frequently brought up topic is pets. I suggest you include a pet addendum and have a detailed policy on pets. Personally, I do not want any pets in my properties. Most pets can cause significant damage, so I'd rather avoid the risk. The specific clause in my lease states that no pets are allowed without written consent by the landlord. If a tenant requests and I approve, there is an additional deposit collected and also $50 added to the rent price. I only consider caged animals, cats or lap dogs.

STEP 6: THE KEYS & FINAL THOUGHTS

The final step in the process is to deliver the keys and begin the tenancy. However, before you do that you should meet your tenant at the property and perform a final walk through. During the walk-through meeting, you should note the condition of the entire property on a tenant move-in report (condition report) and verify that all keys are functioning properly. You and the tenant should agree on the condition of items as well as on the language used to complete the form. As previously mentioned, it is a good idea to take pictures throughout the walk through to accurately and objectively capture everything. The move-in report is a document that will be filed throughout the tenancy and used as documented evidence to support any charges due to damages at the end of the tenancy.

The Keys.

Once completed, now it's time to hand over the keys and allow the tenant to move in. I provide two sets of keys and install new locks at the end of each tenancy. Keys should never be handed over until the lease is signed and all of the deposit money is paid. You should also withhold keys until the property has been cleaned, prepped and is ready for move in. Never hand out keys if renovations are still underway because tenants tend to casually stop by when they have keys in their possession.

As you get your tenants and embark upon your landlording, there are a few operational *keys* to remember. Continue to revise and update your documentation, get comfortable delivering stern messages and always make the smart financial decisions pertaining to your property. Never become too friendly with tenants and blur lines. You must maintain your roles as landlord and tenant. When tenants feel too comfortable, they will tend to push limits and take advantage of your relationship. I have had tenants who pushed capacity limits, delayed payment of rent and snuck pets into the property. You will need to perform routine inspections and take notes and pictures for your inspection reports. Address issues immediately and in a stern manner. Set the stage for appearing in court and be prepared to follow through. If tenants don't comply after a verbal warning, follow up with an eviction letter.

Given the role you must play to protect your business, I advise caution if renting to family. This could be difficult for any landlord to handle but could be especially difficult for newer landlords. Most people find it difficult to muster up the courage to have tough conversations with family or friends, as opposed to a stranger. Also, going in, understand that it can put a strain on the relationship. Whether they have an issue paying rent or neglect their maintenance responsibilities, you must approach the situation with your business hat on and deliver the tough message. Likewise, if they raise an issue about you or your management, you must train yourself to receive it as an objective landlord. But as you can imagine, this can easily create a weird or unfavorable dynamic. Personally, while I don't advise it for everyone, I have rented to friends and family in the past. It can be awkward at times, but I have been able to maintain my position and perform my duties. If you decide to allow friends and family to rent, you must be consistent and do not allow any exception that you wouldn't allow to others. Doing so will only hurt your business and your asset. At the end of the day, if I rent to my mom and I need to evict her, then that's just what I'm going to do (haha I'm only kidding mom, I could never). She may be the only person who'd get exception from me, but you understand the point I'm driving. To be fair, one benefit to renting to family and friends is that you already know them on a personal level. You should have a general idea of their character, their level of responsibility and a good gauge of whether or not they can pay rent with no issue.

Always keep in mind that this is indeed a business, so you must maintain your profitability. Stay plugged in to the market and be diligent about rent price adjustments. Taxes, insurance, and other expenses continue to rise so you will need to raise rent accordingly. Most investors will finance the property, so they will carry a mortgage, homeowner's insurance, utilities and various ongoing maintenance. As a result, most investors will only profit a few hundred dollars from a residential rental property. As a rule, I aim to net $400/month minimum on a property. Thankfully, I have been able to maintain this minimum profitability on most of my projects. In fact, on my first rental property, I cleared over $600 per month in profit. While it's great to set a target, you must also be practical and consider the market trends when setting your rent. For example, winter months are generally slower, which can drive prices down. You will have to consider the fair market rate when setting your rent price so that you are not listing your property too low or too high. Of course, you can't control when your lease ends, but it's still beneficial to consider rental activity since market value will fluctuate.

MY 1st PROPERTY PUCHASE

 **Rental Property**

Success Story Break Down

The strategy behind my first deal was to buy a property that I could both live in as well as rent out. My primary goal was to live for free from the rents, but I was also looking to create positive cash flow as well. This was accomplished beautifully. The property was a 3-story row home that I partitioned into two living spaces. I created a 3rd floor apartment for me and then designated the second floor as a rooming house (renting 3 rooms for $375 a piece).

Purchase Price	$64,900
Down Payment (3.5%) + Closing Costs	$7,522
Seller Assist (6%)	$3,894
Loan Amount	$62,629
Mortgage Payment (includes Taxes & Insurance)	$488
Rehab Costs	$13,650
Total Cash out-of-pocket	$17,278
Monthly Rent	$1,125
Montly Profit	$637

Annual Profit (minus 20% Contingency Loss) = $6,115

MY 1st PROPERTY PUCHASE
Rental Property

Purchase Price: $64,900
Neighborhood: Philadelphia
Bedrooms: 5
Bathrooms: 2.5
Sqft: 2010
Basement: Unfinished
Heating: Gas, Radiator
Notes: Needed updating/TLC

SUCCESS STORY BREAKDOWN

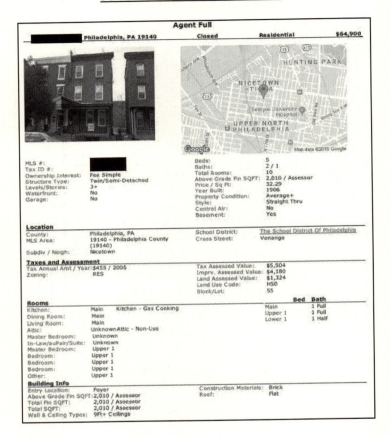

SUCCESS STORY BREAKDOWN

Foundation Details: Stone
Basement Type: Full, Unfinished

Lot
Lot Acres / SQFT: 0.04a / 1,936sf
Lot Size Dimensions: 20X98
Lot Features: Front Yard

Interior Features
Interior Features: Kitchen - Eat-In, No Fireplace, Accessibility Features: None, Basement Laundry

Exterior Features
Exterior Features: Sidewalks, Porch(es)

Parking
Parking: On Street Parking, 0-Car Garage

Utilities
Utilities: No Cooling, Electric Service: 100 Amp Service, Heating: Radiator, Heating Fuel: Natural Gas, Hot Water: Natural Gas, Water Source: Public, Sewer: Public Sewer

Remarks
Inclusions: None
Exclusions: None
Agent: Motivated Sellers - Show and Sell!
Public: Huge 3-story Twin within walking distance to Temple Hospital and the broad street subway. The possibilities are endless for this property as is the potential. The property features 10ft ceilings and alot of old world charm.

Listing Office
Listing Agent:
Listing Agent Email:
Broker of Record:
Listing Office:

Office Phone:
Office Email:

Compensation
Buyer Agency Comp: 3%%
Dual/Var Comm: No

Listing Details
Original Price: $69,900
Previous List Price: $64,900
Vacation Rental: No
Owner Name:
Listing Agrmnt Type: Exclusive Right
DOM / CDOM: 6 / 6
Prospects Excluded: No
Original MLS Name: TREND
Listing Service Type: Full Service
Off Market Date: 04/28/05
Dual Agency: No
Original MLS Number:
Listing Term Begins: 03/08/2005
Listing Entry Date: 03/08/2005
Possession: Immediate
Acceptable Financing: Conventional

Sale/Lease Contract
Selling Agent:
Selling Agent Email:
Selling Office:

Office Phone:
Selling Office Email:
Concessions:
Concession Remarks: Seller assist 6%
Agreement of Sale Dt: 03/08/05
Close Date: 04/28/05
Close Price: $64,900.00
Buyer Financing: Conventional
Last List Price: $64,900.00

Landlording is not for everyone, but it is a proven way to grow enormous wealth. If you are interested in this method of investment, I suggest doing your due diligence and then diving in. Don't be a person who spends too much time researching and preparing before taking action. Whether out of fear or discomfort in the unknown, people will always be able to find excuses to delay or even abandon starting a new venture. Bruce Lee was quoted saying that "if you spend too much time thinking about a thing, that thing will never get done." If this is truly something you want to do, then take massive action and begin your rental empire. Fun fact: survey data by CNBC found that 43 million households in the US were renter-occupied while 75 million were owner-occupied. With over 1/3 of the households in the United States paying rent, there is a lot of money to be made from a good rental property. Learn from your mistakes and the experiences of others. Use this as fuel to push forward smarter. Take action, fail forward and continuously refine your skillset.

END

References

1. https://www.nolo.com/legal-encyclopedia/how-evictions-work-pennsylvania.html
2. https://www.nolo.com/legal-encyclopedia/overview-landlord-tenant-laws-pennsylvania.html
3. https://www.phila.gov/fairhousingcommission/pages/default.aspx
4. https://www.hud.gov/program_offices/fair_housing_equal_opp/fair_housing_act_overview#_The_Fair_Housing
5. https://www.american-apartment-owners-association.org/landlord-tenant-laws/pennsylvania/
6. https://www.landlordology.com/pennsylvania-landlord-tenant-laws/
7. https://realestate.findlaw.com/landlord-tenant-law.html

8. https://www.apartmentguide.com/blog/apartment-guide-annual-rent-report/
9. https://www.rentalprotectionagency.com/rental-statistics.php
10. https://ipropertymanagement.com/renters-vs-homeowners-statistics/
11. https://www.phila.gov/li/pages/tenantlandlord.aspx
12. https://www.mysmartmove.com/SmartMove/blog/6-rental-statistics-landlords-need-know.page

Made in the
USA
Middletown, DE